NATIONAL STRATEGY FOR

INFORMATION SHARING

*Successes and Challenges
In Improving
Terrorism-Related
Information Sharing*

OCTOBER 2007

CONTENTS

INTRODUCTION AND OVERVIEW

Our success in preventing future terrorist attacks depends upon our ability to gather, analyze, and share information and intelligence regarding those who want to attack us, the tactics that they use, and the targets that they intend to attack. Our *National Strategy for Combating Terrorism*, issued in September 2006, recognizes that the War on Terror is a different kind of war, which requires a paradigm shift and the application of all elements of our national power and influence. The intelligence and information sharing structures that once enabled the winning of the Cold War now require greater flexibility and resilience to confront the threats facing our Nation from a transnational terrorist movement determined to destroy our people, our freedoms, and our way of life.

For the past six years, this Administration has worked within the Federal Government, and with our State, local, tribal, private sector, and foreign partners to transform our policies, processes, procedures, and—most importantly—our workplace cultures to reinforce the imperative of improved information sharing. The exchange of information should be the rule, not the exception, in our efforts to combat the terrorist threat. Substantial improvements have occurred within individual agencies and disciplines, but there is still more to be done. Improving information sharing in the post–September 11 world requires an environment that supports the sharing of information across all levels of government, disciplines, and security domains. As with our achievements to date, an improved information sharing environment will not be constructed overnight, but rather will evolve over time and will be the fruit of careful cultivation. An improved information sharing environment also will be constructed upon a foundation of trusted partnerships among all levels of government, the private sector, and our foreign allies—partnerships based on a shared commitment to detect, prevent, disrupt, preempt, and mitigate the effects of terrorism. This *Strategy* sets forth the Administration's vision of what improvements are needed and how they can be achieved.

The *Strategy* was developed with the understanding that homeland security information, terrorism information, and law enforcement information related to terrorism can come from multiple sources, all levels of government, as well as from private sector organizations and foreign sources. Federal, State, local, and tribal government organizations use such information for multiple purposes. In addition to traditional law enforcement uses, such information is used to (1) support efforts to prevent terrorist attacks, (2) develop critical infrastructure protection and resilience plans, (3) prioritize emergency management, response, and recovery planning activities, (4) devise training and exercise programs, and (5) determine the allocation of funding and other resources for homeland security-related purposes.

The Need for a National Strategy

While improved information sharing has been an Administration priority since the September 11 attacks, this *Strategy* reflects the first time the Administration has articulated the full contours of its vision in a single document. Memorializing the *Strategy* in a single document not only provides information to others about the Administration's plans and outlook, but also guides our efforts as we continue to implement many programs and initiatives designed to advance and facilitate the sharing of terrorism-related information.

This *Strategy* will assist the Administration in ensuring that Federal, State, local and tribal government employees responsible for protecting our Nation from future attacks or responding should an attack occur understand the Administration's expectations and plans for achieving improvements in the gathering and sharing of information related to terrorism.

Accordingly, while this *Strategy* describes the vision that has guided the Administration for the past six years, it also sets forth our plan to build upon progress and establish a more integrated information sharing capability to ensure that those who need information to protect our Nation from terrorism will receive it and those who have that information will share it. We will improve interagency information sharing at the Federal level, while building information sharing bridges between the Federal Government and our non-Federal partners.

Guiding Principles

Those responsible for combating terrorism must have access to timely and accurate information regarding those who want to attack us, their plans and activities, and the targets that they intend to attack. That information guides our efforts to:

- Identify rapidly both immediate and long-term threats;

- Identify persons involved in terrorism-related activities; and

- Implement information-driven and risk-based detection, prevention, deterrence, response, protection, and emergency management efforts.

Experience has shown that there is no single source for information related to terrorism. It is derived by gathering, fusing, analyzing, and evaluating relevant information from a broad array of sources on a continual basis. Important information can come through the efforts of the Intelligence Community, Federal, State, tribal, and local law enforcement and homeland security authorities, other government agencies (e.g., the Department of Transportation, the Department of Health and Human Services), and the private sector (e.g., the transportation, healthcare, financial, and information technology sectors). Commonly referred to as homeland security information, terrorism information, or law enforcement information, this wide-ranging information can be found across all levels of government as well as in the private sector.

This *Strategy* provides the vision for how our Nation will best use and build upon the information sharing innovations which have emerged post-September 11 in order to develop a fully coordinated and integrated information sharing capability that supports our efforts to combat terrorism. The *Strategy* is founded on the following core principles and understandings:

- Effective information sharing comes through strong partnerships among Federal, State, local, and tribal authorities, private sector organizations, and our foreign partners and allies;

- Information acquired for one purpose, or under one set of authorities, might provide unique insights when combined, in accordance with applicable law, with seemingly unrelated information from other sources, and therefore we must foster a culture of awareness in which people at all levels of government remain cognizant of the functions and needs of others and use knowledge and information from all sources to support counterterrorism efforts;

- Information sharing must be woven into all aspects of counterterrorism activity, including preventive and protective actions, actionable responses, criminal and counterterrorism investigative activities, event preparedness, and response to and recovery from catastrophic events;

- The procedures, processes, and systems that support information sharing must draw upon and integrate existing technical capabilities and must respect established authorities and responsibilities; and

- State and major urban area fusion centers represent a valuable information sharing resource and should be incorporated into the national information sharing framework, which will require that fusion centers achieve a baseline level of capability to gather, process, share, and utilize information and operate in a manner that respects individuals' privacy rights and other legal rights protected by U.S. laws.

Foundational Elements

This *Strategy* is focused on improving the sharing of homeland security, terrorism, and law enforcement information related to terrorism within and among all levels of governments and the private sector.

- **Information Sharing at the Federal Level.** The instruments of our national power have long depended on the capabilities of the Intelligence Community to collect, process, analyze, and disseminate intelligence regarding our adversaries and enemies. Our efforts to combat terrorism depend on enhancing those intelligence capabilities, while enabling other Federal departments and agencies responsible for protecting the United States and its interests to regularly share information and intelligence with other public and private entities in support of mission critical activities. Information sharing at the Federal level has improved significantly since September 11, but challenges still remain that must be addressed before our strategic vision is realized.

- **Information Sharing with State, Local, and Tribal Entities.** As our Nation's first "preventers and responders," State, local, and tribal governments are critical to our efforts to prevent future terrorist attacks and to respond if an attack occurs. They must have access to the information that enables them to protect our local communities. In addition, these State, local, and tribal officials are often best able to identify potential threats that exist within their jurisdictions. They are full and trusted partners with the Federal Government in our Nation's efforts to combat terrorism, and therefore they must be a part of an information sharing framework that supports an effective and efficient two-way flow of information enabling officials at all levels of government to counter and respond to threats.

- **Information Sharing with the Private Sector.** Private sector information represents a crucial element in both understanding the current threat environment and protecting our nation's critical infrastructure from targeted attacks. The private sector owns and operates over 85% of the nation's critical infrastructure and is therefore a primary source of important vulnerability and other potentially relevant consequence information. Some private sector entities have cultivated effective information sharing partnerships with the State and local authorities that regulate their activities in the localities in which they operate. Important elements of the private sector have made significant investments to develop mechanisms and methodologies to evaluate, assess, and exchange information across regional, market, and security-related communities of interest; however still more can be done to improve those mechanisms and communication. We will use both sector-specific and geographic strategies to ensure effective information sharing with the private sector.

- **Sharing Information with Foreign Partners.** In the immediate wake of the September 11 attacks, many foreign governments joined the United States as partners in the Global War on Terrorism, and many have since contributed to the war in important ways. The events of the past six years have reaffirmed that risks and threats often emerge and take shape without regard to geographic borders. Intelligence provided by foreign partners often provides the first indications of terrorist plans and intentions. Accordingly, we are taking steps to evaluate and improve upon our sharing of information with foreign governments and encouraging them to share with us.

- **Protecting Information Privacy and Other Legal Rights.** It will remain essential to continue to protect the information privacy and other legal rights of Americans as we protect our Nation from terrorism. Accordingly, our efforts will remain relentless on two fronts -- protecting our people, communities, and infrastructure from attack and zealously protecting the information privacy and other legal rights of Americans. At the President's direction, the Attorney General and the Director of National Intelligence developed guidelines that describe how executive departments and agencies will protect the information privacy and other legal rights of Americans when sharing information related to terrorism. Consistent with the *Intelligence Reform and Terrorism Prevention Act of 2004*, the guidelines were developed in consultation with the Privacy and Civil Liberties Oversight Board.

Foundations of the National Strategy for Information Sharing

Linkage with Other National Strategies

The *National Strategy for Information Sharing* does not exist in a vacuum. It is a critical component of our Nation's comprehensive approach for combating terrorism. As such, it takes its lead from the President's *National Security Strategy*, which provides the broad vision and goals for confronting the national security challenges of the 21st century. In addition, it is closely aligned with the *National Strategy for Combating Terrorism* and the *National Strategy for Homeland Security*.

This *Strategy* also supports and supplements the National Implementation Plan, which is the foundational document guiding the efforts of the Directorate of Strategic Operational Planning in the National Counterterrorism Center, required by the *Intelligence Reform and Terrorism Prevention Act of 2004*. The National Implementation Plan integrates the activities of all elements of national power into our efforts to combat terrorism. Additionally, the *Strategy* supports and supplements other relevant planning efforts, such as those associated with the implementation of the National Response Plan and the establishment of a National Command and Coordination Capability.

Finally, this *Strategy* aligns with the *National Intelligence Strategy*, published at Presidential direction by the Director of National Intelligence in October 2005. An information sharing framework is recognized as a critical component of intelligence reform in the *National Intelligence Strategy*.

Background and the Current Environment

One clear lesson of September 11 was the need to improve the sharing of information. To prevent further attacks and to protect the homeland, we need to stay a step ahead of those individuals and organizations intent upon harming America. Key to preventing future attacks is the gathering of information about terrorist risks and threats and then ensuring that the information gets into the hands of those whose responsibility it is to protect our communities and critical infrastructure. In the past six years, we have achieved significant accomplishments in our efforts to improve information sharing, and we are well positioned in the current environment to build upon those past accomplishments as we move forward.

What has been accomplished since the September 11 attacks?

In the aftermath of the September 11 terrorist attacks, our Nation began a historic transformation aimed at preventing future attacks and improving our ability to protect and defend our people and institutions at home and abroad. As a result, we are now better informed of terrorist intentions and plans and better prepared to detect, prevent, and respond to their actions. Improved intelligence collection and analysis have helped paint a more complete picture of the threat, while more information sharing has provided us a greater capacity for coordinated and integrated action.

- We worked with the Congress to adopt, implement, and renew key reforms like the USA PATRIOT Act that remove barriers that once restricted the sharing of information between the law enforcement and intelligence communities, while at the same time protecting our fundamental liberties.

- We established the Department of Homeland Security (DHS) in part to improve the sharing of information among Federal, State, and local government agencies and the private sector, in order to enhance our Nation's ability to detect, identify, understand, and assess terrorist threats to and vulnerabilities of the homeland to better protect our Nation's critical infrastructure, integrate our emergency response networks, and link State and Federal governments.

- We reorganized the Intelligence Community. The position of Director of National Intelligence was created to serve as the President's chief intelligence advisor and the head of the Intelligence Community and to ensure closer coordination and integration of the 16 agencies that make up the Intelligence Community.

- We established the National Counterterrorism Center (NCTC) to serve as a multi-agency center analyzing and integrating all intelligence pertaining to terrorism, including threats to U.S. interests at home and abroad.

- We worked to develop an Information Sharing Environment (ISE) to enhance the sharing of terrorism-related information among Federal, State, local, and tribal governments and the private sector. The President designated a Program Manager for the ISE to lead these efforts. The President also issued guidelines to inform the continued development of the ISE.

- We have worked to achieve the objectives set out in the President's guidelines by devising and instituting various initiatives designed to improve information sharing both at the Federal level and with our partners at the State, local, and tribal level, as well as with our foreign partners, while simultaneously taking great care to ensure that mechanisms are in place to protect the information privacy and other legal rights of Americans.

- We established the Terrorist Screening Center to consolidate terrorist watch lists and provide around-the-clock operational support for Federal and other law enforcement personnel across the country.

- We have provided significant grant funding to support the establishment of State and major urban area information fusion centers. Fusion centers coordinate the gathering, analysis, and sharing of criminal intelligence, public safety information, and other information related to terrorism within specific States or localities. As of September 1, 2007, 58 fusion centers have either been established or are in the process of being established.

- We have brought about significant growth and maturation of the 101 Joint Terrorism Task Forces (JTTF) in major cities throughout the United States. The JTTFs have substantially contributed to improved information sharing and operational capabilities at the State and municipal levels.

- The Attorney General and the Director of the Federal Bureau of Investigation (FBI) have worked with the Director of National Intelligence to create the FBI National Security Branch by merging the FBI Counterterrorism and Counterintelligence Divisions with the newly established Directorates of Intelligence and Weapons of Mass Destruction. Establishment of the Directorate of Intelligence and of Field Intelligence Groups in every FBI field office exemplify the FBI's major steps to transform itself into a preeminent domestic counterterrorism agency.

- The Secretary of Homeland Security has appointed a Chief Intelligence Officer responsible for integrating the intelligence activities of all DHS components.

- We have established the U.S. Northern Command within the Department of Defense (DoD) to plan, organize, and execute military, homeland defense, and civil support missions in the continental United States, Alaska, and offshore waters.

- The National Guard Bureau has completed a major organizational transformation including establishment of the National Guard Bureau Joint Staff focused on Homeland Defense and Defense Support of Civil Authorities mission requirements and the creation of a single Joint Force Headquarters in each of the States and Territories.

- DHS has expanded the Homeland Security Information Network, a computer-based counterterrorism communications network, to all 50 States, five territories, the District of Columbia, and 50 other major urban areas to strengthen the two-way flow of threat information among Federal, State, local, and tribal officials. Additionally, DHS is streamlining and merging its disparate classified networks into a single, integrated network called the Homeland Secure Data Network, to provide classified access to State, local, and tribal governments.

- The Department of State has initiated a Visa and Passport Security Program and Strategic Plan to target and disrupt individuals or organizations worldwide that are involved in the fraudulent production, distribution, or use of visas and passports, or other similar activities, intended to aid unlawful entry into the United States.

- The State Department's Bureau of Diplomatic Security has enhanced the Rewards for Justice Program to encourage reporting to authorities with tips, leads, and other information critical to preventing or favorably resolving acts of international terrorism against U.S. persons or property worldwide.

- The Department of Treasury has worked to upgrade and enhance its classified communications networks to be fully compatible with the Intelligence Community's in order to ensure that information related to terrorist financing and other national security threats related to financial crime are safely and efficiently communicated to and coordinated with the Intelligence Community.

Through these and other efforts, the United States and its coalition partners have made significant strides against al-Qaida, its affiliates, and others who threaten us. Collaboration and information sharing have helped limit the ability of al-Qaida and like-minded terrorist groups to operate successfully. We have uncovered and eliminated numerous threats to our citizens and to our friends and allies. We have disrupted terrorist plots, arrested operatives, captured or killed senior leaders, and strengthened the capacity of the Nation to confront and defeat our adversaries.

Continuing Challenges

We are engaged in what some have termed "a long war," or a "protracted conflict," and our enemy has proved to be adept at evolving and adapting his tactics. Internationally, al-Qaida remains the most serious threat to the Homeland as its central leaderships continues to plan high impact attacks while pushing others in extremist communities to mimic its efforts and supplement its capabilities. Its leadership is being reconstituted, and new jihadists are being recruited and trained daily. Additionally, the spread of radical internet sites, increasingly aggressive anti-U.S. rhetoric and actions, and the growing number of radical, self-generating cells in Western countries indicate that the radical and violent segment of the West's Muslim population is expanding. As a result, the Untied States will continue to face ideologically committed extremists determined to attack our interests at home and abroad.

Serious challenges lie ahead, including defeating the enemy, denying safe haven, combating violent extremist ideologies, and protecting the homeland. For the foreseeable future, those challenges will continue to be a top priority for the Federal Government on all fronts – intelligence, diplomatic, homeland security, law enforcement, and defense.

While these instruments of our national power are mighty, the nature of the global threat, as well as the emergence of homegrown extremists, require that State, local, and tribal governments incorporate counterterrorism activities as part of their daily efforts to provide emergency and non-emergency services to the public. These partners are now a critical component of our Nation's security capability as both "first preventers" and "first responders," and their efforts have achieved concrete results within their communities, as the following examples illustrate:

- A narcotics investigation – conducted by Federal, State, and local law enforcement officials and resulting in multiple arrests – revealed that a Canadian-based organization supplying precursor chemicals to Mexican methamphetamine producers was in fact a Hezbollah support cell.

- A local police detective investigating a gas station robbery uncovered a homegrown jihadist cell planning a series of attacks.

- An investigation into cigarette smuggling initiated by a county sheriff's department uncovered a Hezbollah support cell operating in several States.

To combat and prevent terrorist actions effectively we must first acquire knowledge about their organizations' plans, intentions, and tactics, and then ensure that such knowledge is available to those responsible for preventing and responding to attacks. The Intelligence Community will continue to be a primary source for this information; however, the Intelligence Community must modify its processes and procedures to encompass non-traditional customers at all levels of government with roles in prevention and response. In addition, important information regarding possible attack planning may come from organizations outside the Intelligence Community. Our challenge is to ensure that information from all sources is brought to bear on our efforts to protect our people and infrastructure from terrorist attacks.

Today, the sharing of terrorism-related information takes place within multiple independent sharing environments that serve five communities—intelligence, law enforcement, defense, homeland security, and foreign affairs. Historically, each community developed its own policies, rules, standards, architectures, and systems to channel information to meet mission requirements. These environments were insulated from one another, which resulted in gaps and seams in the sharing of information across all levels of government.

Recognizing these significant challenges, the Congress passed and the President signed the *Intelligence Reform and Terrorism Prevention Act of 2004*. Among other things, the law called for the creation of the ISE to enable trusted partnerships among all levels of government, the private sector, and our foreign partners, in order to more effectively detect, prevent, disrupt, preempt, and mitigate the effects of terrorism against the territory, people, and interests of the United States. This partnership will enable the trusted, secure, and appropriate exchange of terrorism-related information across the Federal Government, to and from State, local, and tribal governments, foreign allies, and the private sector, and at all levels of security classifications.

Through this *Strategy* and the use of the ISE we will:

- Enable greater coordination at the Federal level, so that strategic and time-sensitive threat information gets into the hands of those who need it to protect our local communities and our Nation's interests at home and abroad;

- Facilitate the exchange of coordinated sets of requirements and information needs across the Federal and non-Federal domains to help guide the targeting, selection, and reporting of terrorism-related information;

- Make certain that intelligence products can be easily shared, as appropriate, with those outside the Intelligence Community, such as other Federal entities, State, local, tribal, and foreign governments, and the private sector;

- Enable State, local, and tribal government efforts to gather, process, analyze, and share information and intelligence;

- Establish a network of State and local information fusion centers operating in a manner that safeguards information privacy rights and other legal rights of Americans;

- Ensure our efforts to prevent future terrorist attacks are risk-based, information-driven, and supported by a greater understanding of our adversaries' motivations, intentions, and plans; and

- Change government culture to one in which information is regularly and responsibly shared and only withheld by exception.

Although the effort to implement the ISE is well underway, it is essential for implementation activities to take place within a broader strategic context. The sections that follow describe in more detail the current environment, the key elements of our National *Strategy*, and the actions we will take to achieve our vision.

Legislative and Regulatory Background

On August 27, 2004, the President issued two Executive Orders pertinent to this *Strategy*. Executive Order 13354 established the NCTC as "the primary organization in the United States Government for analyzing and integrating all intelligence possessed or acquired by the United States Government pertaining to terrorism and counterterrorism [with the exception of] purely domestic counterterrorism information." Executive Order 13356 was aimed directly at strengthening the sharing of terrorism information to protect Americans. Specifically, the President directed agencies to give the "highest priority" to the prevention of terrorism and the "interchange of terrorism information [both] among agencies" and "between agencies and appropriate authorities of States and local governments." The President further directed that this improved information sharing be accomplished in ways that "protect the freedom, information privacy, and other legal rights of Americans."

The *Intelligence Reform and Terrorism Prevention Act*, enacted in December 2004, placed NCTC within the newly created Office of the Director of National Intelligence. The law directed NCTC to "serve as the primary organization in the United States Government for analyzing and integrating all intelligence possessed or acquired by the United States Government pertaining to terrorism and counterterrorism." In addition, NCTC serves as "the central and shared knowledge bank on known and suspected terrorists and international terror groups, as well as their goals, strategies, capabilities, and networks of contacts and support." The NCTC strives to ensure that agencies, as appropriate, receive and have access to the intelligence necessary to perform their counterterrorism missions.

Section 1016 of the *Intelligence Reform and Terrorism Prevention Act of 2004* directed the establishment of the ISE, which it defined as "an approach that facilitates the sharing of terrorism information." The President was charged to create the ISE, designate its organization and management structure, and determine and enforce the policies and rules to govern the ISE's content and usage. The law further required the ISE be "a decentralized, distributed, and coordinated environment" that "to the greatest extent practicable, … connects existing systems … ; builds upon existing systems capabilities currently in use across the Government; … facilitates the sharing of information at and across all levels of security; … and incorporates protections for individuals' privacy and civil liberties."

In addition, the law required the President designate a Program Manager for the ISE. The role of the Program Manager is to manage the ISE, oversee its implementation, assist in the development of ISE standards and practices, and monitor and assess its implementation by Federal departments and agencies. The law also established an Information Sharing Council to advise the President and the Program Manager on the development of ISE policies, procedures, guidelines, and standards, and to ensure proper coordination among Federal departments and agencies participating in the ISE.

Accordingly, the President designated the Program Manager and directed that the Program Manager and his staff be located in the Office of the Director of National Intelligence. On October 25, 2005, the President issued Executive Order 13388, superseding Executive Order 13356, to facilitate the work of the Program Manager, expedite the establishment of the ISE, and restructure the Information Sharing Council.

On December 16, 2005, in accordance with section 1016 of the *Intelligence Reform and Terrorism Prevention Act of 2004*, the President issued a Memorandum to Heads of Executive Departments and Agencies prescribing the guidelines and requirements in support of the creation and implementation of the ISE. In the December Memorandum, the President directed that the ISE be established by building upon "existing Federal Government policies, standards, procedures, programs, systems, and architectures (collectively "resources") used for the sharing and integration of and access to terrorism-related information, and … leverage those resources to the maximum extent practicable, with the objective of establishing a decentralized, comprehensive, and coordinated environment for the sharing and integration of such information." He also directed the heads of executive departments and agencies to "actively work to create a culture of information sharing within their respective departments or agencies by assigning personnel and dedicating resources to terrorism-related information sharing, by reducing disincentives to such sharing, and by holding their senior managers accountable for improved and increased sharing of such information."

The President's Memorandum also included five specific guidelines designed to advance the development and implementation of the ISE.

- **Guideline One:** the President directed that common standards be developed "to maximize the acquisition, access, retention, production, use, management, and sharing of terrorism information within the ISE, consistent with the protection of intelligence, law enforcement, protective, and military sources, methods, and activities." These common standards, the President further directed, must accommodate and account for the need to improve upon the sharing of terrorism-related information with State, local, and tribal governments and the private sector.

- **Guideline Two:** the President stressed that "war on terror must be a national effort" and therefore one in which State, local, and tribal governments and the private sector are afforded appropriate opportunities to participate as full partners in the ISE. Accordingly, he directed that a common framework be developed governing the roles and responsibilities of Federal departments and agencies relating to the sharing of terrorism information, homeland security information, and law enforcement information among Federal departments and agencies, State, local, and tribal governments, and private sector entities.

- **Guideline Three:** the President directed a series of actions be undertaken to improve upon the sharing of Sensitive but Unclassified (SBU) information. Specifically, he directed the heads of particular departments and agencies to submit recommendations for the standardization of SBU procedures for marking and handling terrorism information, homeland security information, and law enforcement information, and eventually all other types of information shared within the ISE.

- **Guideline Four:** the President recognized the imperative for the ISE to facilitate and support the appropriate exchange of terrorism information with our foreign partners and allies and, toward that end, directed the development of recommendations to achieve improved sharing in this area.

- **Guideline Five:** the President directed, as he did earlier in Executive Order 13353, that the information privacy rights and other legal rights of Americans must be protected. Accordingly, he required guidelines be developed and submitted for approval to ensure such rights are protected in the implementation and operation of the ISE.

On November 16, 2006, pursuant to the President's delegation of authority, the Director of National Intelligence submitted to the Congress a report containing the *Implementation Plan for the Information Sharing Environment.* The ISE Implementation Plan, among other things, delineates how the President's guidelines and requirements will be implemented by drawing upon recommendations developed pursuant to those guidelines. The plan contains descriptions of the functions, capabilities, resources, and conceptual design of the ISE, a plan for deploying and operating the ISE, and a process for measuring implementation progress and performance. The plan, which is available on the Program Manager's website (www.ise.gov), was developed through a collaborative effort among the Program Manager and the member organizations of the Information Sharing Council. It also incorporates the perspectives of representatives from State, local, and tribal governments who reviewed the ISE Implementation Plan Report during its development. Since the Plan's submission to the Congress, many of its action items have been implemented.

Most recently, the *Implementing Recommendations of the 9/11 Commission Act of 2007*, enacted in August of this year, included amendments to section 1016 of the *Intelligence Reform and Terrorism Prevention Act of 2004* and to the *Homeland Security Act of 2002*. The new law expands the scope of the ISE to explicitly include homeland security information and weapons of mass destruction information. It also endorses and formalizes many of the recommendations developed in response to the President's information sharing guidelines, such as the creation of the Interagency Threat Assessment and Coordination Group, and the development of a national network of State and major urban area fusion centers.

Sharing Information at the Federal Level

Today's ISE consists of multiple sharing environments designed to serve five communities: intelligence, law enforcement, defense, homeland security, and foreign affairs. Our objective is to establish a framework for Federal agencies in the fulfillment of their individual roles and responsibilities and forge a coordinated and trusted interagency partnership and process across all five communities. This collaborative approach at the Federal level will in turn drive the manner in which terrorism-related information is shared with non-Federal partners. Those efforts support and build upon the success of ongoing initiatives at each level of government, offer practical guidance for addressing challenges that emerge, and provide the multi-agency perspective necessary to achieve the objectives of information sharing. In addition, as our information sharing efforts mature, policy and technology will lead to the introduction of additional information sources not currently included or available within those Federal communities.

NCTC has the primary responsibility within the Federal Government for analysis of all intelligence and information pertaining to terrorism, and supports the Department of Justice (DOJ), DHS, and other appropriate agencies in the fulfillment of their responsibilities to disseminate terrorism-related information. To carry out this responsibility, NCTC is staffed by personnel from many Federal departments and agencies, thus allowing the development of coordinated and integrated assessments of terrorist threats, plans, intentions, and capabilities.

NCTC also serves as the central and shared knowledge bank on known and suspected terrorists and international terror groups and ensures that agencies have access to and receive all-source intelligence support needed to execute their counterterrorism plans or perform independent, alternative and mission-oriented analysis. Authorized agencies may request information from NCTC to assist in the agency's activities, consistent with applicable law and guidelines governing access to intelligence. NCTC enables the sharing of a wide spectrum of terrorism intelligence and related information among thousands of users in the Federal counterterrorism community through its production of comprehensive, "federally coordinated," analytical products and its secure web site, NCTC Online.

All Federal departments and agencies that possess or acquire terrorism-related intelligence and information provide access to such information to NCTC for analysis and integration unless prohibited by law or otherwise directed by the President. As the "Federal Fusion Center" responsible "for analyzing and integrating all intelligence pertaining to terrorism and counterterrorism," NCTC works with appropriate Federal departments and agencies to enable the development of "federally coordinated," terrorism-related information products tailored to the needs of Federal entities. Within the NCTC, the new Interagency Threat Assessment and Coordination Group will facilitate the production of "federally coordinated" terrorism-related information products intended for dissemination to State, local, and tribal officials and private sector partners.

Our efforts to improve the sharing of information related to terrorism acknowledge the interdependent and—in some respects—overlapping responsibilities of the elements of government charged with combating terrorism, securing the homeland, and enforcing laws. We will leverage the strength of each and challenge them to collaborate to build an informed, composite understanding of the nature of the threat, strengthening the United States' posture and making us a more productive and effective partner in the effort to combat terrorism.

Sharing Information with State, Local, and Tribal Governments

Guideline 2 of the President's December 16, 2006, Memorandum to Heads of Executive Departments and Agencies directed that a common framework be developed governing the roles and responsibilities of Federal departments and agencies relating to the sharing of terrorism information, homeland security information, and law enforcement information between and among Federal departments and agencies, State, local, and tribal governments, and private sector entities.

The President's guidelines recognized that State, local, and tribal authorities are critical to our Nation's efforts to prevent future terrorist attacks and are the first to respond if an attack occurs. The attacks of September 11 illustrated that foreign terrorists wanting to commit acts of terrorism might live in our local communities and be engaged in criminal or other suspicious activity as they plan attacks on targets within the United States or its territories. At the same time, there is increasing concern regarding the potential threat posed by homegrown terrorists. While lacking formal ties to al-Qaida, these disaffected, radicalized, violent extremists often draw inspiration from al-Qaida and other global terrorist organizations. Whether a plan for a terrorist attack is homegrown or originates overseas, important knowledge that may forewarn of a future attack may be derived from information gathered by State, local, and tribal government personnel in the course of routine law enforcement and other activities.

State, local, and tribal governments carry out their counterterrorism responsibilities within the broader context of their core mission to protect the public's health and safety and to provide emergency and non-emergency services. While State and local officials work to prevent future terrorist attacks, they still must arrest criminals, put out fires, respond to traffic accidents, and deal with a host of public health and safety issues. Success in these endeavors depends on a strong partnership with the public, built on a foundation of communication and trust between local officials and the members of their community. These same partnerships will be used to protect these communities from future attacks by terrorists.

Needs of State, Local, and Tribal Governments

The informational needs of State, local, and tribal entities continue to grow as they incorporate counterterrorism and homeland security activities into their day-to-day missions. Specifically, they require access to timely, credible, and actionable information and intelligence about individuals and groups intending to carry out attacks within the United States, their organizations and their financing, potential targets, pre-attack indicators, and major events or circumstances that might influence State, local, and tribal preventive and protective postures. To implement recommendations developed pursuant to Guideline 2 of the President's Guidelines, and as key participants in the information sharing mission, State, local, and tribal entities are encouraged to undertake the following activities, in appropriate consultation and coordination with Federal departments and agencies:

- Foster a culture that recognizes the importance of fusing information regarding all crimes with national security implications, with other security-related information (e.g., criminal investigations, terrorism, public health and safety, and natural hazard emergency response);

- Support efforts to detect and prevent terrorist attacks by maintaining situational awareness of threats, alerts, and warnings, and develop critical infrastructure protection plans to ensure the security and resilience of infrastructure operations (e.g., electric power, transportation, telecommunications) within a region, State, or locality; and

- Develop training, awareness, and exercise programs to ensure that State, local, and tribal personnel are prepared to deal with terrorist strategies, tactics, capabilities, and intentions, and to test plans for preventing, preparing for, mitigating the effects of, and responding to events.

Authorities at all levels of our federal system must share a common understanding of the information needed to prevent, deter, and respond to terrorist attacks. The common understanding will be achieved through a framework that enables:

- Federal entities to work together to provide information in ways that better meet the needs of State, local, and tribal partners; and

- Information gathered at the State and local level to be processed, analyzed, disseminated, and integrated with information gathered at the Federal level.

We will have an integrated approach that allows Federal agencies to work together to produce and disseminate a federally-validated perspective on available threat information and relies on the efforts of consolidated fusion environments at the State and regional levels.

Interagency Threat Assessment and Coordination Group

To improve the coordination of the sharing of terrorism-related information, as well as to implement recommendations developed in response to the President's December 16, 2005, Memorandum to the Heads of Executive Departments and Agencies, we have established an Interagency Threat Assessment and Coordination Group (ITACG) within the NCTC. Participants in this coordination group include DHS, FBI, members of the Intelligence Community, and State and local representatives. The coordination group will enable the development of "federally coordinated" perspectives on intelligence reports and analytical products regarding terrorist threats and related issues that address the needs of State, local, tribal, and, as appropriate, private sector entities.

The ITACG supports the efforts of NCTC to produce "federally coordinated" terrorism-related information products intended for dissemination to State, local, and tribal officials and private sector partners through existing channels established by Federal departments and agencies by:

1. Enabling the development of intelligence reports on terrorist threats and related issues that represent a "federally coordinated" perspective regarding those threats and issues and that satisfy the needs of State, local, tribal, and private sector entities until such time as the ISE matures organizationally and culturally to satisfy those needs as a normal part of doing business;

2. Providing advice, counsel, and subject matter expertise to the Intelligence Community regarding the operations of State, local, and tribal officials, including how such entities use terrorism-related information to fulfill their counterterrorism responsibilities as part of their core mission of protecting their communities;

3. Enabling the production of clear, relevant, official, "federally coordinated" threat information in a timely and consistent manner;

4. Facilitating the production of "federally coordinated" situation awareness reporting for State, local, tribal, and private sector entities on significant domestic and international terrorism or terrorism-related events that have the potential to have an impact on local or regional security conditions in the United States;

5. Ensuring terrorism-related information intended for State, local, tribal, and private sector entities is rendered in a usable format that is, to the extent possible, unclassified, to facilitate further dissemination;

6. Informing and helping to shape Intelligence Community products for State, local, tribal, and private sector entities by providing advice, counsel, and subject matter expertise; and

7. Facilitating the production and posting by NCTC of "federally coordinated" terrorism-related information intended for augmentation, as appropriate, and subsequent dissemination to State, local, tribal, and private sector entities by other Federal departments and agencies. Accordingly, the ITACG will advise the Intelligence Community on how to tailor its products to satisfy the needs of DHS, FBI, and other Federal entities so that they in turn can better serve their consumers.

The efforts of the ITACG complement and supplement existing analytic, production, and dissemination efforts by Federal entities. The location at NCTC affords the coordination group direct access to experts assigned to NCTC and other co-located organizations such as the National Joint Terrorism Task Force to effect decisions rapidly regarding sanitization and release of information to be shared with State, local, and tribal officials, and the private sector.

Specifically, the group will coordinate the production and timely issuance of the following interagency products intended for distribution to State, local, and tribal officials, the private sector, as well as the general public when appropriate:

- Alerts, warnings, and notifications of time-sensitive terrorism threats to locations within the United States;

- Situational awareness reporting regarding significant events or activities occurring at the international, national, State, or local levels; and

- Strategic assessments of terrorist risks and threats to the United States.

State and Major Urban Area Fusion Centers

Many State and major urban areas have established information fusion centers to coordinate the gathering, analysis, and dissemination of law enforcement, homeland security, public-safety, and terrorism information. As of September 1, 2007, over 58 of these centers are operating or are being established in States and localities across the country. A majority operate under national guidelines developed through the Global Justice Information Sharing Initiative and Homeland Security Advisory Council. (The full text of the Fusion center Guidelines can be found at www.ise.gov.)

State and major urban area fusion centers are vital assets critical to sharing information related to terrorism. They will serve as the primary focal points within the State and local environment for the receipt and sharing of terrorism-related information. As a part of this *Strategy*, the Federal Government is promoting that State and major urban area fusion centers achieve a baseline level of capability and become interconnected with the Federal government and each other, thereby creating a national, integrated, network of fusion centers to enable the effective sharing of terrorism-related information. The Federal Government will support the establishment of these centers and help sustain them through grant funding, technical assistance, and training to achieve a baseline level of capability and to help ensure compliance with all applicable privacy laws. This approach respects our system of federalism and strengthens our security posture.

Federal departments and agencies will provide terrorism-related information to State, local, and tribal authorities primarily through these fusion centers. Unless specifically prohibited by law, or subject to security classification restrictions, these fusion centers may further customize such information for dissemination to satisfy intra- or inter-State needs. Fusion centers will enable the effective communication of locally generated terrorism-related information to the Federal Government and other fusion centers through the ISE. Locally generated information that is not threat- or incident-related will be gathered, processed, analyzed, and interpreted by those same fusion centers—in coordination with locally based Federal officials—and disseminated to the national level via the DoD, DHS, FBI, or other appropriate Federal agency channels. Where practical, Federal organizations will assign personnel to fusion centers and, to the extent practicable, will strive to integrate and collocate resources.[1]

---

[1] Appendix 1 delineates the specific roles and responsibilities of Federal, State, local, and tribal governments as they relate to the establishment and continued operation of State and major urban area fusion centers and provides guidelines to support the performance of those roles and responsibilities.

SHARING INFORMATION WITH THE PRIVATE SECTOR

As the terrorist attacks on transportation infrastructure in London and Madrid demonstrate, critical infrastructure can be a prime target for the transnational terrorist enemy we face today. The private sector owns and operates an estimated 85% of infrastructure and resources that are critical to our Nation's physical and economic security. It is, therefore, vital to ensure we develop effective and efficient information sharing partnerships with private sector entities. Important sectors of private industry have made significant investments in mechanisms and methodologies to evaluate, assess, and exchange information across regional, market, and security-related communities of interest. This *Strategy* builds on these efforts to adopt an effective framework that ensures a two-way flow of timely and actionable security information between public and private partners.

Efforts to improve information sharing with the private sector have initially focused on sharing with the owners and operators of our Nation's critical infrastructure and key resources. In accordance with the National Infrastructure Protection Plan, we are currently implementing a networked approach to information sharing that allows distribution and access to information both horizontally and vertically using secure networks and coordination mechanisms, allowing information sharing and collaboration within and among sectors. It also enables multi-directional information sharing between government and industry that focuses, streamlines, and reduces redundancy in reporting to the greatest extent possible.

These processes are enabling the integration of private sector security partners, as appropriate, into the intelligence cycle and National Common Operating Picture. Moreover, sector security partners are becoming more confident that the integrity and confidentiality of their sensitive information can and will be protected and that the information sharing process can produce actionable information regarding threats, incidents, vulnerabilities, and potential consequences to critical infrastructure and key resources. These efforts are being integrated into broader efforts to establish the ISE.

It is important to note that critical infrastructure and key resource owners and operators utilize a number of mechanisms that facilitate the flow of information, mitigate obstacles to voluntary information sharing, and provide feedback and continuous improvement regarding structure and process. These include the Sector Coordination Councils, Government Coordination Councils, National Infrastructure Coordinating Center, Sector-level Information Sharing and Analysis Centers (commonly referred to as ISACs), DHS Protective Security Advisors, the DHS Homeland Infrastructure Threat and Risk Analysis Center (HITRAC), and State and major urban area fusion centers. These mechanisms accommodate a broad range of sector cultures, operations, and risk management approaches and recognize the unique policy and legal challenges for full two-way sharing of information between private sector owners and operators and government, as well as the important requirements for efficient operational processes.

Our efforts to improve information sharing with the private sector have been guided by a number of important factors:

- Current, reliable, accurate, and actionable information is critical to private sector decisions to protect their business;

- Private sector entities gather, process, analyze, and share information in order to protect their companies' assets, employees, infrastructure, and ability to operate, so as to maintain a competitive advantage;

- In many cases, private sector entities have spent years establishing strong working relationships with Federal, State, and local law enforcement and other entities; this *Strategy* respects and encourages those established relationships;

- The private sector operates within multiple information sharing frameworks: industry executives often prefer to separately share threat-related information with Federal and State as well as local government officials and other business executives as they assess the threat environment in which they operate, implement protective measures, and engage in emergency response planning activities;

- As we incorporate the information sharing needs and capabilities of the private sector into our efforts to enable information sharing, we need to recognize that at times the environment in which homeland security, law enforcement, and terrorism-related information is shared mirrors the regulatory environment in which the sharing entity operates; and

- The private sector relies on multiple information sources including professional and local organizations, private information providers, news outlets, colleagues, open intelligence sources on the web, and company management in both domestic and foreign locations, in addition to the government at all levels (Federal, State, and local).

Accordingly, as we improve efforts to share terrorism-related information with the private sector we must continue to:

- Build a trusted relationship between Federal, State, local, and tribal officials and private sector representatives to facilitate information sharing;

- Improve the two-way sharing of terrorism-related information on incidents, threats, consequences, and vulnerabilities, including enhancing the quantity and quality of specific, timely, and actionable information provided by the Federal Government to critical infrastructure sectors and their State, local, and tribal partners;

- Ensure that Federal, State, local, and tribal authorities have policies in place that ensure the protection of private sector information that is shared with government entities;

- Integrate private sector analytical efforts into Federal, State, local, and tribal processes, as appropriate, for a more complete understanding of the terrorism risk; and

- Establish mechanisms and processes to ensure compliance with all relevant U.S. laws, including applicable information privacy laws.

We will continue to build upon existing successful information sharing partnerships in a variety of areas key to our national security. Those include programs such as the following:

- The Critical Infrastructure Partnership Advisory Council – provides the framework for owner and operator members of Sector Coordinating Councils and members of Government Coordinating Councils to engage in intra-government and public-private cooperation, information sharing, and engagement across the entire range of critical infrastructure protection activities;

- InfraGard – a partnership between the Federal Government, an association of businesses, academic institutions, State and local law enforcement agencies, and other participants dedicated to sharing information and intelligence to prevent hostile acts against the United States;

- Protected Critical Infrastructure Information/Sensitive Security Information – an information-protection tool that facilitates information sharing between the government and the private sector, which is used by DHS and other Federal, State, and local analysts in pursuit of a more secure homeland, focusing primarily on analyzing and securing critical infrastructure and protected systems, identifying vulnerabilities and developing risk assessments, and enhancing recovery preparedness measures;

- The Overseas Security Advisory Council – a Federal advisory committee that promotes security cooperation between American business and private sector interests worldwide and currently encompasses the 34-member core Council, an Executive Office, over 100 Country Councils, and more than 3,500 constituent member organizations and 372 associates; and

- Existing collaborative information sharing relationships between private sector entities and State and local authorities to facilitate the sharing of time-sensitive threat and vulnerability information, which reflect the preference, in some cases, of private sector entities to coordinate the sharing of threat-related and other information with the government authorities responsible for regulating their activities.

The President also created the National Infrastructure Advisory Council (NIAC). The NIAC is charged to make recommendations on improving the cooperation and partnership between the Federal Government and industry, for the purpose of securing the critical infrastructures. The advice from the NIAC is meant to assist the President and the Secretary of Homeland Security in the development of policies and strategies that range from risk assessment and management to information sharing, protective measure, and clarification on roles and responsibilities between public and private sectors.

Finally, the needs and capabilities of the private sector, particularly those entities considered to be critical infrastructure or key resources, will be incorporated into efforts to establish a national, integrated network of State and major urban area fusion centers and to produce "federally coordinated" terrorism-related information products at NCTC.

Sharing Information with Foreign Partners

Strong and effective cooperation with our foreign partners is a vital component of the global war on terrorism. The President recognized the need to share information with foreign partners in his December 16, 2005, Memorandum to the Heads of Executive Departments and Agencies. Accordingly, the sharing of terrorism-related information between Federal departments and agencies and foreign partners and allies forms a critical component of our information sharing strategy.

The counterterrorism mission requires sharing many types of terrorism-related information, for example, the exchange of biographic and biometric information related to known or suspected terrorists. While such sharing often includes classified information and sensitive diplomatic, law enforcement, and homeland security information relating to terrorism, it also encompasses other information that, over time, may help reveal links to terrorist groups or individuals. Information regarding lost or stolen passports and suspect financial transactions, for example, might yield information on groups or persons who subsequently are linked to a specific terrorist threat. In addition to asking for such information from other countries, it is also essential that we appropriately share similar types of information with foreign governments or foreign law enforcement entities, such as INTERPOL, as long as the sharing of any records about American citizens and lawful permanent residents data is subject to the *Privacy Act of 1974* limitations, especially regarding personally identifiable information.

Information sharing with foreign partners is a key component of international outreach and cooperation to protect U.S. critical infrastructure. Given the often sensitive nature of the information shared, we will continue to enter into agreements and other understandings with foreign governments to ensure appropriate security and confidentiality of exchanged information. We must also expect that foreign governments will seek the same assurances from us. As a general rule, such agreements and understandings should seek sufficient security of information while also permitting flexible handling of the exchanged information to allow practical use. We must strive to ensure that safeguarding and handling restrictions are calibrated to maximize both the quantity and quality of information shared with, or received from, a foreign government. To the maximum extent possible, we will adopt and adhere to commonly accepted and standard safeguarding and handling restrictions.

There is the basic requirement that shared information be appropriately safeguarded and protected from public disclosure. Our foreign partners at times may ask us to agree to particular restrictions on the dissemination or use of the information. While it is preferable to avoid such restrictions, it may be necessary in certain circumstances to accept some limitations as a condition for receiving information with particularly high value. How we proceed in such situations will depend on the circumstances presented and our need for the information at issue. Our guiding objective will be to ensure that information received from a foreign government can be disseminated as broadly as possible and used for critical counterterrorism purposes.

Similar challenges arise in regard to sharing information with foreign governments that may contain personal data about United States citizens and permanent residents. In particular, the *Privacy Act of 1974* confers certain protections upon information concerning citizens and lawful permanent residents. Accordingly and especially given considerations of reciprocity, we must remain sensitive to the potential impact on our citizens and lawful residents of sharing information involving U.S. persons with foreign partners. The United States must carry out its counterterrorism mission while also ensuring that appropriate protection of information regarding our citizens and lawful permanent residents. As part of approving the recommendations submitted to improve information sharing with foreign governments, the President directed that the potential impact on United States persons be considered when evaluating a proposed information sharing arrangement with a foreign government.

Special considerations present themselves in the area of sharing classified information with foreign governments. Such sharing will continue to occur in a relatively formal context, to account for the need to properly secure and limit disclosure of the information. Indeed, decisions of whether to share our Nation's classified information are extraordinarily sensitive and will be made with the utmost care. Our officials must remain cognizant of the imperative to our national security mission of maximizing the sharing of terrorism-related information, while also taking care to ensure that sharing arrangements do not result in the unintended compromising of our national security.

In summary, strong partnerships and trusted collaboration with foreign governments are essential components of the war on terror. Effective and substantial cooperation with our foreign partners requires sustained liaison efforts, timeliness, flexibility, and the mutually beneficial exchange of many forms of terrorism-related information. The strategic objectives for sharing information with foreign partners can be broadly summarized as follows:

- Expanding and facilitating the appropriate and timely sharing of terrorism-related information between the United States and our foreign partners;

- Ensuring that exchanges of information between the United States and foreign governments are accompanied by proper and carefully calibrated security requirements;

- Ensuring that information received by Federal agencies from a foreign government under a sharing arrangement: (1) is provided to appropriate subject matter experts for interpretation, evaluation, and analysis; and (2) can be disseminated and used to advance our Nation's counterterrorism objectives;

- Refining and drawing upon sets of best practices and common standards in negotiating sharing arrangements with foreign governments; and

- Developing standards and practices to verify that sharing arrangements with foreign governments appropriately consider and protect the information privacy and other legal rights of Americans.

Protecting Privacy and Other Legal Rights in the Sharing of Information

Protecting the rights of Americans is a core facet of our information sharing efforts. While we must zealously protect our Nation from the real and continuing threat of terrorist attacks, we must just as zealously protect the information privacy rights and other legal rights of Americans. With proper planning we can have both enhanced privacy protections and increased information sharing – and in fact, we must achieve this balance at all levels of government, in order to maintain the trust of the American people. The President reaffirmed this in his December 16, 2005, Memorandum to the Heads of Executive Departments and Agencies.

At the direction of the President, the Attorney General and the Director of National Intelligence developed a set of Privacy Guidelines to ensure the information privacy and other legal rights of Americans are protected in the development and use of the ISE. The Privacy Guidelines provide a consistent framework for identifying information that is subject to privacy protection, assessing applicable privacy rules, implementing appropriate protections, and ensuring compliance. An array of laws, directives, and policies provide substantive privacy protections for personally identifiable information. The parameters of those protections vary depending on the rules that apply to particular agencies and the information they are proposing to share. As described below, however, the Guidelines demand more than mere compliance with the laws; they require executive departments and agencies to take pro-active and explicit actions to ensure the balance between information privacy and security is maintained, as called for by the *National Commission on Terrorist Attacks Upon the United States*. The full text of the ISE Privacy Guidelines can be found at www.ise.gov.

Core Privacy Principles

The Privacy Guidelines build on a set of core principles that Federal departments and agencies must follow. Those principles require specific, uniform action and reflect basic privacy protections and best practices. Agencies must:

- Share protected information only to the extent it is terrorism information, homeland security information, or law enforcement information related to terrorism;

- Identify and review the protected information to be shared within the ISE;

- Enable ISE participants to determine the nature of the protected information to be shared and its legal restrictions (e.g., "this record contains individually identifiable information about a U.S. citizen");

- Assess, document, and comply with all applicable laws and policies;

- Establish data accuracy, quality, and retention procedures;

- Deploy adequate security measures to safeguard protected information;

- Implement adequate accountability, enforcement, and audit mechanisms to verify compliance;

- Establish a redress process consistent with legal authorities and mission requirements;

- Implement the guidelines through appropriate changes to business processes and systems, training, and technology;

- Make the public aware of the agency's policies and procedures as appropriate;

- Ensure agencies disclose protected information to non-Federal entities—including State, local, tribal, and foreign governments—only if the non-Federal entities provide comparable protections; and

- State, local, and tribal governments are required to designate a senior official accountable for implementation.

Privacy Governance

Successful implementation of the Privacy Guidelines requires a governance structure to monitor compliance and to revise the Guidelines as we gain more experience. The President, therefore, directed the Program Manager to establish the ISE Privacy Guidelines Committee. The Committee is chaired by representatives of the Attorney General and the Director of National Intelligence, and consists of the Privacy Officials of the departments and agencies of the Information Sharing Council. The Committee seeks to ensure consistency and standardization, as well as serve as a forum to share best practices and resolve agency concerns.

INSTITUTIONALIZING THE STRATEGY
FOR LONG-TERM SUCCESS

Over the past six years we have made significant improvements in the way that terrorism-related information is shared. There remains more we can and must do to ensure that those responsible for protecting our people, interests, and infrastructure have the information they need to carry out their mission. Individual departments and agencies of the Federal Government have been directed to work together to ensure that Federal information and intelligence capabilities are brought together to form a national assured information sharing capability. These same individual departments and agencies have been directed to work together to ensure that State and major urban area fusion centers are interlinked with each other and Federal information and intelligence capabilities to form a national information sharing capability. This *Strategy* provides the vision of how we will build upon the progress of the past six years and establish an integrated information sharing capability to ensure that those who need information to protect our Nation from terrorism receive it and that those who have information share it.

The preceding sections of this *Strategy* described the four areas of information sharing and the overarching need to ensure that our efforts to expand the sharing of terrorism-related information are accompanied by adequate protections for information privacy rights and other rights guaranteed by the Constitution and laws of the United States. The challenge is to ensure that those areas, and the guiding principles on which they are based, are incorporated in a framework of specific, measurable activities that guide the development and implementation of the ISE and increase the sharing of terrorism-related information across the Federal Government and with State, local, tribal, and private sector entities and our foreign partners.

Ultimately, implementing this *Strategy* will create a powerful national capability to share, search, and analyze terrorism-related information that spans jurisdictional, organizational, and cultural boundaries and provides users a distributed, secure, and trusted environment for transforming data into actionable information. It also takes advantage of the vital roles played by State and major urban area information fusion centers, which are crucial investments for improving the nation's analytical capacity.

This *Strategy* is being institutionalized through many actions including the following:

The ISE Implementation Plan Report – In November 2006, the Director of National Intelligence produced and provided to the Congress a report containing an Implementation Plan for the ISE that outlines almost 100 specific actions and supporting recommendations for achieving the goals for the ISE, as envisioned in the *Intelligence Reform and Terrorism Prevention Act of 2004* and in Executive Order 13388.

This plan reflects the culmination of collaboration between the Program Manager, the Information Sharing Council, and Federal departments and agencies. It also incorporates the perspectives of representatives from State, local, and tribal governments who reviewed the ISE Implementation Plan Report during its development.

Sharing with State, Local, and Tribal Governments and the Private Sector

The Interagency Threat Assessment and Coordination Group – The Administration established an Interagency Threat Assessment and Coordination Group at the national level to better coordinate the sharing of terrorism-related information. The Group will facilitate the production of what will be officially defined as "federally coordinated" terrorism-related information products intended for dissemination to State, local, and tribal officials and private sector partners through the established channels. As noted previously, the Group will include representatives from DHS, FBI, and other relevant Federal entities as well as State and local government representatives. The Group will ensure that both classified and unclassified intelligence produced by Federal entities within the intelligence, law enforcement, and homeland security communities is fused, validated, de-conflicted, and approved for dissemination in a concise and, when possible, unclassified format.

State and Major Urban Area Fusion Centers – We will improve collaboration at the State and local levels by leveraging State and major urban area information fusion centers and by establishing a national integrated network of these centers. Appendix 1 delineates the specific roles and responsibilities of State and major urban area fusion centers.

Collocation of personnel from State and major urban area fusion centers and local JTTFs, Field Intelligence Groups, and National Guard intelligence units is also encouraged.

Through the Federal grants process and related technical assistance and training efforts, the Federal Government is working to ensure that these centers achieve and maintain a baseline level of operational and analytical capability by encouraging the adoption of the Global Justice Information Sharing Initiative/Homeland Security Advisory Council Fusion Guidelines and by expanding the amount of technical assistance and training provided.

Sharing with Our Foreign Partners and Allies

Standard International Agreement Text – We are developing standard language on information sharing and protection that can be used in international agreements pertaining to terrorism-related information sharing to facilitate agreement on a level of protection that would not unnecessarily impede re-dissemination for counterterrorism purposes.

Central Repository – We are establishing a central, electronically accessible repository of information on foreign government and international organization marking and handling regimes so that U.S. agencies and domestic partners can more readily understand safeguarding and handling rules for different kinds of foreign government information.

Protecting the Information Privacy and Legal Rights of Americans

ISE Privacy Guidelines – The ISE Privacy Guidelines are designed to establish a framework for sharing terrorism-related information in the ISE in a manner that protects privacy and civil liberties. These guidelines require agencies to identify any privacy-protected information to be shared and they put in place accountability mechanisms, audit mechanisms, and redress procedures.

ISE Privacy Officials – The Guidelines require Federal departments and agencies to designate an "ISE Privacy Official" to directly oversee implementation of the Guidelines.

ISE Privacy Guidelines Committee – The Guidelines also provide for an ISE Privacy Guidelines Committee, consisting of the ISE Privacy Officials of the Federal departments and agencies that are members of the Information Sharing Council, and chaired by a senior official designated by the Program Manager of the ISE.

Appendix 1
Establishing a National Integrated Network of State and Major Urban Area Fusion Centers

Roles and Responsibilities of Federal, State, Local, and Tribal Authorities

Roles of the State and Major Urban Area Fusion Centers

Federal, State, local, and tribal governments have specific responsibilities as it relates to the establishment and continued operation of State and major urban area fusion centers. The roles and responsibilities outlined in this *Strategy* were developed in partnership with State, local, and tribal officials and represent a collective (Federal, State, local, and tribal) view. This *Strategy* recognizes the sovereignty of State and local governments, and thus the roles and responsibilities are delineated with the understanding that State and major urban area fusion centers are owned and managed by State and local governments. Furthermore their incorporation into the ISE takes into account that these centers support day-to-day crime control efforts and other critical public safety activities. Interlinking and networking these centers will create a national capacity to gather, process, analyze, and share information. Incorporating these centers into the ISE will be done in a manner that protects the information privacy and other legal rights of Americans and corporations, as provided for under U.S. law.

The Federal Government may need to provide financial and technical assistance, as well as human resource support, to these fusion centers if they are to achieve and sustain a baseline level of capability. The objective is to assist State and local governments in the establishment and the sustained operation of these fusion centers. A sustained Federal partnership with State and major urban area fusion centers is critical to the safety of our Nation, and therefore a national priority.

State and major urban area fusion centers will be the focus, but not exclusive points, within the State and local environment for the receipt and sharing of terrorism information, homeland security information, and law enforcement information related to terrorism. These fusion centers support the efforts of State, local, and tribal entities in undertaking the following activities and responsibilities, in appropriate consultation or coordination with Federal departments and agencies:

- Share classified and unclassified information to address domestic security and criminal investigations with other States, localities, regions and the Federal Government in a manner that protects the information privacy and other legal rights of Americans, while ensuring the security of the information shared.

- Foster a culture that recognizes the importance of fusing "all crimes with national security implications" and "all hazards" information (e.g., criminal investigations, terrorism, public health and safety, and emergency response) which often involves identifying criminal activity and other information that might be a precursor to a terrorist plot.

- Support critical counterterrorism, homeland security, and homeland defense-related activities, including but not limited to the development or maintenance of:

  1. Mechanisms to contribute information of value to ongoing Federal terrorism risk assessments;

  2. Statewide, regional, site specific, and topical risk assessments;

  3. Processes in support of information responsive to federally communicated requirements and tasks;

  4. Alerts, warnings, notifications, advisories, and/or bulletins regarding time sensitive or strategic threats;

  5. Situational awareness reports; and

  6. Analytical reports regarding geographically relevant incidents or specific threats.

- Develop, in coordination with Federal authorities, critical infrastructure protection plans to ensure the security and resilience of infrastructure operations (e.g., electric power, transportation, telecommunications, water) within a region, State, or locality. The efforts of State and major urban area fusion centers in this regard will be coordinated with information sharing activities delineated in the National Infrastructure Protection Plan as well as other efforts already underway by DoD, DHS, FBI, and other Federal entities.

- Prioritize emergency management, response, and recovery planning activities based on likely threat scenarios and at-risk targets.

- Provide assessments of risk that support State and urban area homeland security preparedness planning efforts to allocate funding, capabilities, and other resources.

- Provide risk-related information to support efforts to develop training, awareness, and exercise programs to ensure that State, local, and tribal officials are prepared to deal with terrorist strategies, tactics, capabilities, and intentions and to test plans for preventing, preparing for, mitigating the effects of, and responding to events.

- Further customize federally supplied information for dissemination to meet intra- or inter-State needs, unless specifically prohibited or otherwise subject to additional security restrictions.

- Ensure that all locally generated terrorism-related information—including suspicious activity and incident reports—is communicated to the Federal Government and other States, localities, and regions, through the appropriate mechanism and systems. Locally generated information that does not appear to be threat or incident related will be gathered, processed, analyzed, and interpreted by the same State and major urban area fusion centers in coordination with locally-based Federal officials. The same information will be disseminated to the national level via appropriate Federal agencies.

Federal, State, Local, and Tribal Responsibilities

I. General

Federal Responsibilities

The Federal Government, in coordination with State, local, and tribal officials, will establish a working group of the Information Sharing Council, to coordinate Federal efforts to support the creation of a national network of State and major urban area fusion centers. Drawing upon existing and ongoing efforts at the Federal level, DoD, DOJ, DHS, the Office of the Director of National Intelligence, and National Guard Bureau shall establish a coordinated set of policies, protocols, and procedures to:

1. Develop, maintain and, as appropriate, disseminate an assessment of terrorist risks and threats to the United States and it interests.

2. Use risk and threat assessments to identify and gather information responsive to the identified threats and risks.

3. Gather and document the information needs of State, local, and tribal governments.

4. Continue to develop a prioritized listing of informational products needed by State, local, and tribal governments based on terrorism information requirements.

5. Maintain existing analytical resources capable of producing (researching, developing, drafting and packaging) these analytical products and coordinating both their development and dissemination.

6. Identify any gaps in production capabilities as it relates to the production of: alerts, warning and notifications regarding time sensitive threat, situational awareness reporting regarding significant events, strategic assessments of threats posed by individuals or terrorist organizations, tradecraft utilized by organizations, geographic risk assessments, or other related issues.

7. Mitigate production gaps by leveraging existing departmental, agency, or NCTC analytical capabilities.

8. Maintain the capability to produce and coordinate multi-channel dissemination of inter-agency coordinated alerts, warnings, and notifications of time sensitive terrorism-related information.

9. Support State, local, and tribal efforts to produce State, regional, and site-specific risk assessments by adopting common terminology and criteria and providing State and local officials an agreed upon assessment methodology for evaluating risk (threat, consequence, and vulnerability).

10. Coordinate the assignment of representative personnel to State and major urban area fusion centers and otherwise strive to integrate and, to the extent practicable, collocate resources.

11. Ensure the sharing of information is done in a manner that protects the information privacy and legal rights of Americans.

State, Local, and Tribal Responsibilities

Each State will be encouraged to define and document how it intends to carry out intrastate efforts to gather, process, analyze, and disseminate terrorism information, homeland security information, and law enforcement information. This process is commonly known as the "fusion process." Defining this process should include the following:

1. In those States where there exist multiple fusion centers, one fusion center, with the demonstrated capacity to serve as the statewide center or hub, should be designated as the primary interface with the Federal Government. This statewide fusion center should also coordinate the gathering, processing, analysis, and dissemination of homeland security information, terrorism information, and law enforcement information on a statewide basis.

2. The Executive Agent of each Urban Area Security Initiative (UASI), as well as the applicable State's homeland security advisor, must work together to determine the most effective manner in which to incorporate the UASI into the statewide information sharing framework.

3. In those instances in which the UASI has established a regional fusion center, the activities of the major urban area fusion center should be incorporated into the statewide fusion process.

4. Each State and major urban area fusion center is encouraged to coordinate with the appropriate Federal authorities to develop synchronized protocols for sharing information with the private sector.

II. Achieving and Sustaining Baseline Operational Standards for State and Major Urban Area Fusion Centers

Federal Responsibilities

The Federal Government, working in partnership with State, local, and tribal authorities, will seek to define the current national information sharing capability that exists through the existence of existing State and major urban area fusion centers. State and local authorities will be asked to support these efforts by assessing and documenting the baseline level of capability of their existing fusion centers.

The Federal Government, in consultation with State, local, and tribal authorities, shall compile, document, and disseminate baseline operational standards, the achievement of which will determine whether an individual State or major urban area fusion center is considered to have achieved a baseline level of capability. These baseline operational standards will build on the Global Justice Fusion Center Guidelines. Additionally, the Federal Government will initiate a series of activities to assist State and major urban area fusion centers to adopt and incorporate these baseline operational standards into their business operations. These standards will support the gathering, processing, analysis, and dissemination of terrorism information, homeland security information, and law enforcement information. Specific Federal activities include:

1. Defining, documenting, and disseminating the baseline operational standards.

2. Assessing the existing level of capability of each designated State and major urban area fusion center.

3. Providing technical assistance, training, and other support as needed by these fusion centers to support their achieving the defined baseline level of capability.

4. Amending relevant grants guidance and technical assistance to ensure that fusion center grant recipients, as a condition of receiving funding, meet delineated baseline operational standards.

5. Modifying grants, other applicable funding programs, and related technical assistance programs to support efforts to sustain the capacity of State and major area fusion centers to operate at a baseline operational level once achieved.

6. Establishing a best practices clearing house capability for fusion centers to include creating a list of Subject Matter Experts.

7. Developing a coordinated interagency approach that supports, wherever practical, the assignment of Federal personnel to State and major urban area fusion centers and otherwise strive to integrate and, to the extent practicable, collocate resources.

State, Local, and Tribal Responsibilities

State, local, and tribal authorities are encouraged to take the following steps to ensure that State and major urban area fusion centers achieve and sustain a baseline level of capability:

1. Support efforts to complete an assessment of existing capabilities within designated State and major urban area fusion centers.

2. Identify and document capability gaps (if any) and develop a strategy and investment plan to mitigate any capability gaps.

3. Track and report efforts to mitigate any capability gaps.

4. Develop an investment strategy to sustain fusion center operations, including a delineation of current and recommended future Federal versus non-Federal costs.

5. Document and report a strategy for integrating State and major urban area fusion center efforts with those of other Federal, State, local, tribal, and private sector information sharing and counterterrorism efforts.

III. Suspicious Activities and Incident Reporting

Federal Responsibilities

The Federal Government will develop a plan and provide State and major urban area fusion centers a mechanism to gather and report locally generated information to appropriate Federal entities, other States, and localities. This locally generated information will include reports by the public or governmental personnel regarding suspicious incidents, events, and activities. Specific activities include:

1. Providing reports and awareness training to State, local, and tribal authorities regarding the strategic goals, operational capabilities, and methods of operation utilized by international and domestic terrorist organizations so that local events and behaviors can be viewed within the context of potential terrorist threats.

2. Developing a prioritized listing of the specific types of locally generated information of interest to Federal entities responsible for assessing the national threat environment and which supports the rapid identification of emerging terrorist threats.

3. Identifying resources capable of communicating and updating these information requirements to State, local, and tribal officials via State and major urban area fusion centers.

4. Establishing a unified process to support the reporting, tracking, processing, storage, and retrieval of locally generated information.

5. Ensuring that efforts to gather, process, analyze, and store locally generated information are carried out in a manner that protects the privacy and legal rights of Americans.

State, Local, and Tribal Responsibilities

State and major urban area fusion centers will support the gathering of locally generated terrorism information, homeland security information, and law enforcement information related to terrorism. Specific activities may include:

1. Completion of a statewide and/or regional risk assessment (threat, vulnerability, and consequence).

2. Using this assessment to identify priority information requirements.

3. Identification of data sources and repositories of prioritized information.

4. Maintaining an information gathering and reporting strategy utilizing existing local capabilities.

5. Developing, implementing, and maintaining a method for communicating information priorities to local gatherers of information.

6. Ensuring that the processes and protocols for ensuring that priority information, including Suspicious Incident Reports (SIRs) and Suspicious Activities Reports (SARs), are disseminated to and evaluated by appropriate government authorities and appropriate critical infrastructure owners and operators.

7. Ensuring that the processes and protocols for ensuring that priority information, including SIRs and SARs, are reported to national entities to support its inclusion into national patterns and trends analysis and other States and localities to support regional trends analysis.

8. Identifying system requirements that support a unified process for reporting, tracking, and accessing SIRs and SARs.

9. Defining a feedback mechanism.

IV. Alerts, Warnings, and Notifications

Federal Responsibilities

The Federal Government, in coordination with State, local, and tribal authorities, will establish processes to manage the issuance of alerts, warnings, and notifications to State and major area fusion centers regarding time sensitive threats and other information requiring some type of State and/or local reaction or response. Specific activities include:

1. Documenting the types of informational products needed by State, local, and tribal governments and the format in which they are desired.

2. Identifying the Federal entities responsible for producing (researching, developing, drafting, and packaging) alerts, warning, and notifications for dissemination to State and major area fusion centers regarding time sensitive threats and coordinating both their development and dissemination.

3. Identifying any gaps in production capabilities as it relates to the production of: alerts, warnings, and notifications regarding time sensitive threats or other related issues.

4. Maintaining the capability to mitigate production gaps by leveraging existing departmental, agency, or NCTC analytical capabilities.

5. Coordinating inter-agency production and multi-channel dissemination of "federally coordinated" alerts, warnings, and notifications of time sensitive threats through the efforts of the Interagency Threat Assessment and Coordination Group.

6. Providing a communications platform, where needed, to transmit alerts, warnings, or notifications, and ultimately consolidating such communications platforms as agreed to through collaborative Federal, State, and local planning and deliberation.

State and Local Responsibilities

State and major urban area fusion centers are encouraged to ensure that alert notifications are disseminated as appropriate, to State, local, and tribal authorities, the private sector and the general public. Specific activities may include:

1. Implement a protocol to govern the receipt of federally generated threat, warning, and notification messages.

2. Develop and/or maintain a plan (processes, protocols, and communication methodology) to govern the further dissemination of federally generated threat, warning, and notification messages, bulletins and other information products to State, local, and tribal authorities, the private sector and the general public.

3. Develop and/or maintain a plan (processes, protocols, and communication methodology) to govern the gathering, processing, and reporting to Federal entities any actions taken by State, local, and tribal authorities and the private sector in response to federally generated threat, warning, and notification messages.

4. Identify and establish a communications platform to support the dissemination of these messages and information products.

5. Coordinate with the appropriate Federal authorities to develop synchronized protocols for sharing information with the private sector.

V. Situational Awareness Reporting

Federal Responsibilities

The Federal Government, in coordination with State, local, and tribal authorities, will establish processes to manage the reporting to key officials and the public information regarding significant events (local, regional, national, and international) that may influence statewide or local security conditions, which include:

1. Documenting the types of informational products needed by State, local, and tribal governments and the format in which they are desired.

2. Identify existing resources capable of producing (researching, developing, drafting, and packaging) these situational reports and coordinating both their development and dissemination.

3. Identify any gaps in production capabilities as it relates to the production of situational awareness reporting regarding significant events.

4. Maintain the capability to mitigate production gaps by leveraging existing departmental, agency, or NCTC analytical capabilities to produce terrorism-related situational reports.

5. Coordinate inter-agency production and multi-channel dissemination of "federally coordinated" situational awareness reports through the efforts of the Interagency Threat Assessment and Coordination Group.

6. Identifying and establishing a communications platform to support the dissemination of such reporting.

State and Local Responsibilities

State and major urban area fusion centers are encouraged to develop the processes to manage the reporting to key officials and the public information regarding significant events (local, regional, national, and international) that may influence State or local security conditions. Such actions may include:

1. Establishing and/or maintaining a protocol to govern the receipt of federally generated situational awareness reports.

2. Establishing and/or maintaining a plan (processes, protocols, and communication methodology) to govern the further dissemination of Federal situational awareness reports and those resulting from media reports to State, local, and tribal authorities, the private sector, and the general public.

3. Establishing and/or maintaining a plan (processes, protocols, and communication methodology) to govern the gathering, processing, and reporting to Federal entities any actions taken by State, local, and tribal authorities and the private sector in response to significant events.

4. Establishing and/or maintaining a protocol to govern the timely reporting of significant events occurring within State or local jurisdictions to Federal authorities and, when appropriate, other States, localities, and regional entities.

5. Coordinating with the appropriate Federal authorities to develop synchronized protocols for sharing information with the private sector.